Frontline Women:

Warriors, Overcomers and Disciples

Dr. Jacquelyn Hadnot

Contents

Frontline Women: Warriors, Overcomers & Disciples

Acknowledgements

This book is dedicated to Apostle Janice Grier and the women of New & Living Way International in Atlanta Georgia.

Your 2014 conference has inspired me to write this book as an encouragement to the women who are armed and ready on the frontline for the Kingdom of God.

Apostle Janice, you are a phenomenal woman and a true inspiration to everyone who is blessed by your presence. Thank you for allowing me to be a part of this move of God. I pray that every assignment you are given reaps an abundant harvest.

Women of New & Living Way International, allow this year's conference to encourage, inspire and push you into your frontline assignment for the Kingdom of God. It is time for the Deborah's and Esther's to arise and walk in victory.

To every woman who picks up this book, I pray that your journey into destiny reaps an abundant harvest because I believe that you are strong enough to endure every obstacle that crosses your path. You have been tried in the fire and come out as pure gold. You have rested at the feet of the Master and received the impartation of His anointing, power and presence.

Kingdom women: warriors, overcomers and disciples, let's get suited and armored for the battle.

Introduction

Greetings, frontline women of God. This book is written just for you. Why? Because you are kingdom women with a kingdom assignment and it is my prayer that this book will help you accomplish great things in the earth. Each assignment is unique to *"the called"* Kingdom woman. Just as no two women are alike, no two assignments are alike. There may be similarities, but our assignments are unique to the divine design of God.

The journey to our individual assignments may be similar, but our paths and the roads we take are unique and specific to our expected end. To complete our assignments we must be armed and prepared for whatever the enemy throws at us.

We must be prepared to stand, command and follow the directions from the Lord, while armed with the full armor of God against the wiles of the devil.

As with any warrior, we must be trained for the battle and equipped with every tool necessary to be victorious. We must possess three vital attributes that epitomize a frontline woman. We must be **warriors** in the spiritual and in the natural realms. We must walk as **overcomers** through the trials by fire. Finally, we must be **disciples** with the ability to walk in discipline and instruction of the Lord.

Frontline women, it is time to get suited, booted and stand shoulder-to-shoulder, arms locked, and ready for our Kingdom assignments. **Attention!**

Frontline Women:

Warriors, Overcomers and Disciples

Dr. Jacquelyn Hadnot

Igniting the Fire Publishing

Frontline Women: Warriors, Overcomers & Disciples

Chapter 1

What is a Frontline Woman?

What is a frontline woman? A frontline woman is a woman who has been called to stand and take lands, territories and nations for the Kingdom of God. A frontline woman has been through more aspects of spiritual warfare than the average person will ever encounter. A frontline woman is a woman who has been tried in the fire and emerged like pure gold. A frontline woman has endured the trial of her faith and brought glory and honor to the Lord. A frontline woman has matured spiritually, mentally and emotionally and she understands what it means to be tried in the furnace of affliction.

What a frontline woman is NOT! The Lord is looking for a vessel to pour out His spirit. He cannot pour His spirit into a bootleg or bastard. He is looking for a broken spirit and a contrite heart. He is looking for a vessel that is naked, broken and unashamed to stand for Him.

What makes a frontline woman a warrior? She knows how to stand, command and walk in the authority given to her by Christ Jesus. She is not afraid to walk in her Kingdom authority and she is not intimidated by anything or anyone. She has faced insecurity, inferiority, low self-esteem and devaluation and walked away stronger, wiser and with a resolute sense of who she is in the Lord.

What makes a frontline woman an overcomer? She knows that regardless of the depths of her pain, she was not built to break and her strength is directly tied to her relationship with the Lord. She knows that her trials were not designed to destroy her; they were intended to strengthen and purify her. She also knows that every adversity that was thrown her way was a tool the Lord used to prepare her for the Master's use.

What is the key to her ability to advance in every area? The fact that she has been discipled at the feet of Jesus. A frontline woman possesses the ability to be strong yet silent, powerful and at the same time walk in humility. She can walk **in** authority while at the same time submit **to** authority. Frontline women are unique to the divine design of the Lord. She is focused, determined and confident in her Commander and Chief. A frontline woman knows that no assignment is too small or too difficult and she faces each assignment with a spirit of determination, excellence and expectation.

It is time to journey deeper into the subject of what it means to be a warrior, overcomer and disciple of the Lord. It is time to discover what it means to be a frontline woman of the Lord.

Chapter 2

The Warrior Woman

As kingdom women, we must wear many hats. One of our hats is that of a warrior. What is a warrior? A warrior is a fighter: *somebody who takes part in or is experienced in warfare.* Therefore, a warrior woman is a woman who is experienced in warfare. A warrior woman is a woman who takes part in a struggle or conflict. She does not run away from the struggles that she encounters. She faces every struggle and trial head on with a holy determination to bring glory to the Kingdom of God. She faces the trials of life without fear or reservation. A warrior woman will go into battle and stand flat-footed waiting for the Lord to bring her victory.

She is a woman dressed in the full armor of God and she never leaves home without being fully prepared and dressed for any situation. She wears the armor of God with fear and reverence for the Lord. She knows that the weapons of her warfare are not physical weapons of flesh and blood, but they are mighty before God for the overthrow and destruction of strongholds. (2 Corinthians 10:4 paraphrased). She also knows that she must be strong in the Lord and be empowered through her union with Him because she draws her strength from Him and His strength is matchless

(Ephesians 6:10 paraphrased).

The warrior woman is equipped like a modern day Deborah and stands ready to engage the battle. Also like Deborah, she knows what it means to lead; *"Deborah, a prophetess, the wife of Lappidoth, was leading Israel at that time"* (Judges 4:4 KJV). Are you called by God to lead an army and take back the things that the enemy has stolen from the people of God? As the Lord spoke to David when Ziklag was attacked, He is speaking to us today and telling us to advance and recover all.

NOW WHEN David and his men came home to Ziklag on the third day, they found that the Amalekites had made a raid on the South (the Negeb) and on Ziklag, and had struck Ziklag and burned it with fire, and had taken the women and all who were there, both great and small, captive. They killed no one, but carried them off and went on their way. So David and his men came to the town, and behold, it was burned, and their wives and sons and daughters were taken captive. Then David and the men with him lifted up their voices and wept until they had no more strength to weep. David's two wives also had been taken captive, Ahinoam the Jezreelitess and Abigail, the widow of Nabal the Carmelite. David was greatly distressed, for the men spoke of stoning him because the souls of them all were bitterly grieved, each man for his sons and daughters. But David encouraged and strengthened himself in the Lord his God. David said to Abiathar the priest,

*Ahimelech's son, I pray you, bring me the ephod. And Abiathar brought him the ephod. And David inquired of the Lord, saying, Shall I pursue this troop? Shall I overtake them? The Lord answered him, Pursue, for you shall surely overtake them and without fail **recover all** (1Samuel 30:8 emphasis added).*

Our ability to stand and command was given to us by the Lord. The Lord's power and authority flows through our veins. Every step we take is done through the power of the Lord. A frontline woman recognizes that she is not operating under her own strength. She knows that it is not by might nor by power, but by the Spirit of the living God that she is able to heal the sick, raise the dead and cast out demons (Zechariah 4:6 paraphrased). Now that you know what it means to be a frontline woman, let's look at the battle array of a Kingdom woman.

The Battle Array of a Warrior Woman

A woman who is well trained in the art of spiritual warfare is a woman who possesses the ability to stand and command. She is not afraid to engage the battle because she knows that the battle is not hers, it belongs to the Lord.

She is a woman of prayer who possesses the strengths of a prayer warrior. She is dressed and armed with the full armor of God and she does not leave her home without her armor fully activated. You will recognize a warrior woman by her battle array and it is grounded in Ephesians chapter 6.

Finally, my brethren, be strong in the Lord, and in the power of his might. Put on the whole armour of God that ye may be able to stand against the wiles of the devil. For we wrestle not against flesh and blood, but against principalities, against powers, against the rulers of the darkness of this world, against spiritual wickedness in high places. Wherefore take unto you the whole armour of God that ye may be able to withstand in the evil day, and having done all, to stand. Stand therefore, having your loins girt about with truth, and having on the breastplate of righteousness; And your feet shod with the preparation of the gospel of peace; Above all, taking the shield of faith, wherewith ye shall be able to quench all the fiery darts of the wicked. And take the helmet of salvation, and the sword of the Spirit, which is the word of God: Praying always with all prayer and supplication in the Spirit, and watching thereunto with all perseverance and supplication for all saints.

- ❖ She is strong in the Lord (v 10).
- ❖ She is strong in the power of His might (v 10).
- ❖ She wears the whole armor of God (v 11).
- ❖ She knows how to stand (v 13-14).
- ❖ She has girt her loins with truth (v 14).
- ❖ She wears the breastplate of righteousness (v 14).
- ❖ She has her feet shod with the preparation of the gospel of peace (v 15).
- ❖ She wears the shield of faith (v 16).
- ❖ She wears the helmet of salvation (v 17).

❖ She carries the sword of the spirit (v 17)

❖ She prays in the spirit (v 18).

❖ She watches in prayer (v 18).

Because you are a heavily armed praying Kingdom woman, you have the ability to:

❖ Stand against every enemy (v 11-14).

❖ Withstand all attacks (v 13).

❖ Quench all the fiery darts of Satan (v 16).

Imagine being on the frontline and missiles and grenades are being launched. You must use your shield to deflect every missile that is launched against you. Darts are deflected because you are covered in the breastplate of righteousness. Your feet are covered with the gospel of peace as you walk through land mines that have been strategically placed to distract you. Your loins are gird (bind, fixed, tightened) with truth so that you won't believe the lies of the enemy. The helmet of salvation covers your head so your mind is focused on the Lord and His voice is the only voice that guides your path. You carry the sword of the spirit, to offensively defend the gospel, and wield the word with precision as you rightly divide the Word of Truth. Finally, as a warrior woman, you are covered in a mantle of prayer and you realize that every word, warning or blessing you receive from the Lord will come to you through prayer.

Are you a warrior woman? Can you stand and command? Are you covered in the mantle of authority? Is the Lord calling you to lead a Kingdom army in this season? If He is calling you, it is time to stand and walk in the Kingdom authority that He has endowed you with. It is time to stand as a modern day Deborah and watch the Lord bring great victories through your life.

You are a kingdom warrior with a kingdom assignment. Everything you have gone through has prepared you for this moment. This is the day that you look at your past and shout with a voice of triumph, "I am an overcomer by the blood of the Lamb and this is my testimony."

Chapter 3

The Overcoming Woman

"They overcame him by the blood of the Lamb and by the word of their testimony" (Revelation 12:11). How many times have you quoted this scripture without giving thought to a deeper meaning as it applies to the victories in your life? How many times have you walked through the fire and furnace of affliction and lived to tell about it? Did you ever stop to think that every

trial was in the divine plan of the Lord to bring you to a place of strength and maturity? Can you look back at every trial, tribulation, and shout, "*I don't look like what I've been through? I may be battered, I may be bruised, but I don't look like what I've been through.*"

The Word of God tells us *that the genuineness of our faith may be tested, our faith which is infinitely more precious than the perishable gold which is tested and purified by fire. This proving of our faith is intended to redound* (have particular results) *to our praise and glory and honor when Jesus Christ (the Messiah, the Anointed One) is revealed* (1 Peter 1:7 paraphrased).

Take a moment and write out a list of the obstacles you have overcome. You will be surprised at the insurmountable odds that were raging against you and yet you stood in the midst of it all. I am making this statement based on the fact that when we are in the middle of our personal tsunamis we cannot see the end of the storm, and as a result, the storm looks bigger than anything we have ever encountered. Have you ever been in the middle of catching hell and suddenly the gates of hell expanded and a new devil and new level was released against you? If you have not, keep living, that day will come. For every trial that you went through, there was a victory waiting on the other side.

In the middle of your valley, there was a mountain top waiting on the horizon. Do you recall the song entitled, *Rough Side of the Mountain*? The singers cry out, *"You don't have to move my mountain, just give me the strength to climb."* I was singing that verse one morning in my best praise and worship voice and the Lord gently said, *"I didn't tell you to climb the mountain, I told you to speak to the mountain."* Allow me to hook you up for free. **Overcomers do not climb the mountains in their lives, they speak to the mountains and the mountains move.** Overcomers see problems as opportunities for victory and a chance to give glory to God.

Overcomers have characteristics and attributes that are unmistakable. An overcomer can be in the middle of the worst warfare in history and you would never know it. Why? Because they refuse to give the enemy any territory. Overcomers give no place to the devil and they shut the enemy down at every opportunity. The Kingdom of heaven *has endured violent assault, and overcomers seize it by force as a precious prize—a share in the heavenly kingdom is sought with most ardent zeal and intense exertion* (Matthew 11:12 AMP paraphrased).

Earlier I asked you to write out a list of the trials you have overcome. Pause for a moment and think back on the times when you thought you were in the worse storm of your life. Think back to the seasons when all hell was breaking loose and you thought the enemy was going to destroy you. Do you remember the times when you thought your life was about to come to an end? Go back to the day when you thought that there was no hope at the end of your rope.

As you reflect on these trying times, use the journal space on the next few pages and write out the adversity you endured and then write out how you were able to ride out the storm and see the

SON shine on the horizon as you walked the road to victory. If possible, include the month and year of the devastating tsunami and then the approximate time you saw the mountain move out of your way. This will help you appreciate the sunshine because you will be able to see the severity of the storm. Nothing helps us appreciate our good times like acknowledging the bad times. The testimony of triumph is like icing on the cake that gives glory and delight to God.

It was not the good times that made us strong; it was the bad times that gave us the strength to endure. It was the bad times that gave strength to our spiritual legs and increased our ability to stand through greatest trials and rise above the darkest storms. Your personal hurricanes, tsunamis, tornadoes and mountains gave you the strength necessary to go the distance with a renewed mindset. It takes a renewed mind to reach your expected end.

It is time to put your pen to paper and bring glory to the Lord by recognizing and appreciating the storm for what it was - the tool that the Lord used to strengthen you for your destiny. Strength comes to anyone who is willing to exercise their spiritual muscles. Are you willing to exercise your spiritual muscles in order to advance for the Kingdom of God? It is time to journal your way to become a stronger, wiser more powerful overcomer.

This exercise in victory has a several purposes:

- To allow you to see the victory at the end of your struggle.

- To allow healing to begin in any desolate areas and shed light on dark places.

- To strengthen you for the next journey and

give you new strategies.

- To reveal your strength as a tried woman.

Victory Journal

_____
_____
_____
_____
_____
_____
_____
_____
_____
_____
_____
_____
_____
_____
_____
_____
_____
_____
_____
_____
_____
_____
_____
_____
_____
_____
_____
_____

_____

_____

_____

_____

_____

_____

_____

_____

_____

_____

_____

_____

_____

_____

_____

_____

_____

_____

_____

_____

_____

_____

_____

_____

_____

_____

_____

_____

_____

The Overcoming Woman

_____

_____

_____

_____

_____

_____

_____

_____

_____

_____

_____

_____

_____

_____

_____

_____

_____

_____

_____

_____

_____

_____

_____

_____

_____

_____

_____

_____

_____

_____

_____
_____
_____
_____
_____
_____
_____
_____
_____
_____
_____
_____
_____
_____
_____
_____
_____
_____
_____
_____
_____
_____
_____
_____
_____
_____
_____
_____
_____

The Overcoming Woman

_____
_____
_____
_____
_____
_____
_____
_____
_____
_____
_____
_____
_____
_____
_____
_____
_____
_____
_____
_____
_____
_____
_____
_____
_____

I hope this exercise in victory has helped you appreciate the trials you have faced. From this day forward, I pray that you will face each challenge with a determination to walk victoriously. Allow a battle cry to flow from your belly that shakes the foundations of the enemy's camp. Your battle cry should resonate, "I am not built to break, and I know the Lord is my strength."

One of the most powerful tools for healing and deliverance is journaling past your pain. Some of your deepest healings will come through journaling. Over the years, I have found journaling to be both therapeutic and resolving. Resolution comes when we open our hearts to the possibilities found in facing our deepest hurts and fears.

Your destiny is tied to your ability to overcome every obstacle. The greater the adversity, the greater the victory. The refiner's fire burns away the residue and debris of your pains and adversities. When the residue has been swept away, what remains is a purified heart that is ready to share a glorious testimony with the world. The journey of an overcomer will never be an easy journey, but it will be one of the most rewarding journeys the world has ever known.

The Bible tells us that we will have trouble on every side of life, but we are fortified through our faith and trust in Christ Jesus. Second Corinthians 4:8 sounds the battle cry of an overcomer who is being pressed by the trials of life. *"We are hedged in (pressed) on every side troubled and oppressed in every way, but not cramped or crushed; we suffer embarrassments and are perplexed and unable to find a way out, but not driven to despair. I am pursued (persecuted and hard driven), but not deserted [to stand alone]; we are struck down to the ground, but never struck out and destroyed."*

What is Second Corinthians telling us?

- ➤ We are pressed on every side, troubled, and oppressed in every way.
  - ➤ *But we are not cramped or crushed.*

- ➤ We suffer embarrassments and are perplexed and unable to find a way out.
  - ➤ *But we are not driven to despair.*

- ➤ We are pursued (persecuted and hard driven), but not deserted [to stand-alone]; we are struck down to the ground.
  - ➤ *But never struck out or destroyed.*

The journey of an overcomer will be shaped with suffering, but it is through the suffering that you will come to know the Lord in the fellowship of His suffering and in the power of His resurrection. As overcomers who often face trouble, we must declare with a resounding voice, *"For my determined purpose is that I may know Him, that I may progressively become more deeply and intimately acquainted with Him, perceiving and recognizing and understanding the wonders of His Person more strongly and more clearly. That I may in that same way come to know the power out flowing from His resurrection which it exerts over believers. That I may share His sufferings as to be continually transformed in spirit into His likeness even to His death, in the hope and if possible I may attain to the spiritual and moral resurrection that lifts me out from among the dead even while in the body"* (Philippians 3:10-11 AMP paraphrased).

> *Who comforts (consoles and encourages) us in every trouble (calamity and affliction), so that we may also be able to comfort (console and encourage) those who are in any kind of trouble or distress, with the comfort (consolation and encouragement) with which we ourselves are comforted (consoled and encouraged) by God (2 Corinthians 1:4).*

Who comforts, consoles and encourages us in every trouble? The Lord Jesus Christ is our comforter and consoler. When He is in our midst, there is no stopping us. He gives us the ability to overcome any flood, wind or rain. He gives us the ability to dance in the midst of the rain. His strength flowing through us gives us the ability to become rain dancers.

Can You Stand the Rain?
The Rain Dance of an Overcomer
"The storms of life are not there to destroy you, allow them to strengthen you."

Let's face it; storms are a part of life. Good or bad, young or old, rich or poor—storms are no respecter of persons. It rains on the just and the unjust. The deciding factor through it all is how you go through the storm. You have two choices, you can go through the storm murmuring and complaining or you can go through the storm learning life's lessons that will help you weather future storms. Complaining only makes your storm worse. Imagine being in the midst of your own personal tsunami with no way out and the only thing you can think of is giving up. Every depressing thought that you have ever had will come to mind when you are in the storm.

Distracting thoughts will also arise when you are in the midst of your most devastating storm. Fear, doubt, negativity, unbelief and the like will throw themselves at you when you are in the midst of a storm. The enemy wants to stop you from dancing, singing, smiling and even living. The result, life becomes a burden with no hope in sight. Remember, life is not about waiting for the storm to pass, it is about learning to dance in the midst of the storm. If you can dance your way through the storm, the storm won't seem so horrendous because your focus will not be on the storm. Your focus will be on how you got THROUGH THE STORM.

When the Disciples were in the boat, their focus

was not on Jesus, their focus was on the storm. When you take your eyes off the Lord, the storm will seem like the most destructive thing you have ever encountered. Try keeping your eyes on the One who can calm every storm in your life. TRY JESUS!

Your ability to overcome the storm is related to your ability to keep your focus on the Storm Calmer as He speaks to the torrential storms in your life. When He says, *"Peace, be still"* and the winds of your storm obey His every command, that is the day that you will know that your storm is over and the promised rainbow of His presence is about to appear before your eyes.

You can begin the rain dance of an overcomer because the stormy days are over, the clouds are passing you by and the SON shine is about to shine in and through your life. You stood the rain, passed the test and His light is now shining on your ways. Know that the Lord has given you perfect peace from the battle that was raging against you. It is time to celebrate and dance the rain dance of an overcomer. Kick your shoes off, pull your hair back, and put on your celebratory music and DANCE! Dance with a reckless abandon that cries, *"I don't have a care in the world because the SON shine is shining brilliantly in my life. I am an overcomer and this is my dance of victory!"* This is the dance and testimony of an overcomer. My sisters, I sincerely hope you dance through your storm.

The Strengths of an Overcomer

Overcomers possess unique strengths that enable them to stand and withstand. Their strength begins and ends with their faith and trust in God. Everything else is a matter of maturity and growth. Some of their strengths include:

- Trust and belief in God
- Faith in God
- Prayer
- Determination
- Perseverance and strength to endure
- The power to press for the goal
- Attitude of gratitude for the trials
- Ability to forgive
- Ability to relax, relate and release
- Ability to look at every obstacle as an opportunity for growth
- Ability to face adversity head on
- Determination to seek resolution to problems

The strengths of an overcomer are always growing and going to greater heights and deeper depths. One thing is for sure, you cannot keep an overcomer down. One day they may appear to be down for the count, but give them a moment and about fifty feet and watch the rise of an overcomer, it is truly a remarkable sight. Much of an overcomer's ability to persevere comes from the fact that they have been tried in the fire and know what it means to suffer for the cause of Christ. Are you a discipled woman?

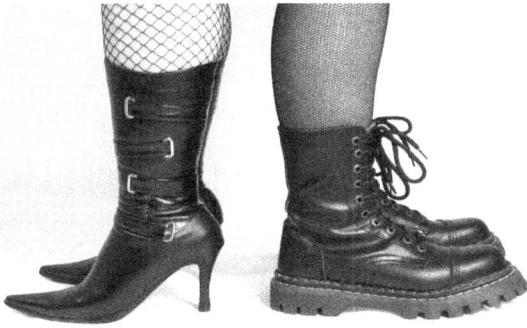

Chapter 4

The Discipled Woman

What is a disciple? A disciple *is somebody who believes in and follows the teachings of a leader, a philosophy, or a religion.* In the *Great Commission*, we are charged to go into all the world and make disciples of all nations.

In the Bible, the disciples were the twelve original followers of Jesus. Are there disciples today? Yes, and as believers in Jesus Christ we must strive to be discipled through the churches or ministry leaders that cover us. Someone was charged with the commission to make a disciple of us and it is our charge to make disciples of others.

When you find a person in a leadership position that has not been discipled or mentored, you will find someone that has missed one of the most important parts of ministry - submitting to and learning from leadership. You will also find bootlegs, renegades, lone rangers and individuals with an unteachable spirit. These individuals are some of the most ineffective people you will ever encounter. These renegades will wreak havoc in any business, ministry or other environment because they do not function well with others. They are not team players. When things don't go their way they take their toys and stomp off pouting and angry. Discipleship training will alleviate some of their questionable people skills.

Discipleship training is equivalent to sitting at the feet of the Master and learning His ways. Our ability to be successful in ministry, business, government or any of the cultural mountains revolves around being properly discipled.

Hans Kvalbein wrote an article on the subject of discipleship that outlines several criteria for effective discipleship. The Themelios article will enable us to be strategic and effective as we walk out discipleship. Kvalbein gives us thirteen theses that outline the New Testament disciple. I have chosen six (6) theses that I believe will help women see their role in being a disciple as well as properly disciplining others.

1. Disciple means learner or student.[1]

2. A disciple learns by (a) hearing his Master, and (b) doing like his Master.[2]

3. The call to be a disciple meant in Jesus' lifetime to leave family, profession and property.[3] (*Please note that this radical demand is viewed as unthinkable in our modern day churches*).

4. To be a disciple is to be called to make new disciples.[4] (*We must be a part of fulfilling the "great commission" otherwise we are not truly His disciples*).

5. The disciples were chosen by *Jesus.*[5] (*As women on the frontline we must know that we are "the called" of God*).

6. The disciples have fellowship with Christ in life and death and are the inheritors of the Kingdom of God.[6] (*We must partake in*

intimate fellowship with the Master if we are to learn His ways).

If we use Kvalbein's theses as our roadmap for discipleship, we will walk in another level or dimension of Christ's power. This can clearly be seen in Matthew 28: 18-20:

"All authority has been given to Me in heaven and on earth. "Go therefore and make disciples of all the nations, baptizing them in the name of the Father and the Son and the Holy Spirit, teaching them to observe all that I commanded you; and lo, I am with you always, even to the end of the age."

There are aspects of Matthew 28 that must be conveyed if you are to receive the fullness of the message Jesus was conveying to His disciples.

1. *"All authority has been given to Me in heaven and on earth."* Jesus is conveying His declaration of power to His disciples.

2. *"Go therefore and make disciples of all the nations.* This is the goal of our commission. *"…baptizing them in the name of the Father and the Son and the Holy Spirit, teaching them to observe all that I commanded you."* This is the means by which other disciples are made.

3. *"I am with you always, even to the end of the age."* This is the promise that He would never leave us nor forsake us as we carry out the work that He has set before us.

Proper discipleship will produce men and women equipped with the essential tools to carry out their Kingdom assignments.

Eight Essentials of a Discipled Woman

There are eight essentials of a discipled woman, without them you will not possess the ability to excel or succeed.

- ❖ Submission: *a willingness to yield or surrender to somebody*

- ❖ Passion: *strong liking or enthusiasm for a subject or activity*

- ❖ Character: *qualities that make somebody or something interesting or attractive*

- ❖ Integrity: *the quality of possessing and steadfastly adhering to high moral principles or professional standards*

- ❖ Discipline: *training to ensure proper behavior*

- ❖ Vision: *an image or concept in the imagination*

- ❖ Strength: *emotional toughness: the necessary qualities required to deal with stressful or painful situations*

❖ Excellence: *a feature or respect in which somebody or something is superior and outstanding*

A properly discipled woman will walk in the attributes of the Master and will not stray from the tenets of His Word. A discipled woman will possess the discipline needed to stand and withstand the tricks, traps and snares that come in her direction. In other words, a discipled woman will walk in the discipline required to be effective in every area of life. A thoroughly disciplined woman will possess the strength to endure every trial, tribulation, situation and circumstance. A disciplined woman will not fall prey to the bait of Satan due to pride, arrogance, lustful impulses, and the like.

In order to understand what makes a disciple, we must understand the meaning of discipline.

Discipline is one of the primary elements needed for growth and development. A disciple without proper discipline is an accident waiting to happen. It is sad to see individuals going into business or ministry without proper discipleship. The Bible tells us in Hebrews 12:6, *"For the Lord corrects and disciplines everyone whom He loves, and He punishes, even scourges, every son whom He accepts and welcomes to His heart and cherishes."* Discipline will come through many forms, but regardless of the manner in which we receive it, we must not resist, hinder or deny discipline. As I stated in an earlier chapter, the Lord is looking for a vessel to pour out His spirit. He cannot pour His spirit into a bootleg or bastard. He is looking a broken spirit and a contrite heart. He is looking for a vessel that is naked, broken and unashamed to stand for Him.

He is looking for a vessel that will endure discipline when it is needed.

What is discipline? Discipline is:

1. **Training to ensure proper behavior:** the practice or methods of teaching and enforcing acceptable patterns of behavior.

   In order to be successful in any endeavor, a discipled woman must have the necessary training to ensure proper behavior. Training comes when we submit to the authority of leadership. A well discipled woman knows how to submit to authority and gain the knowledge from headship that will enable her to advance in every area.

2. **Order and control:** a controlled orderly state.

I was taught that order comes before the anointing. In other words, we must have a firm grasp on the need for order and control if our endeavors are to be successful. Otherwise, chaos will erupt in everything we attempt. We will have drama popping out all over the place, nothing will be accomplished, and God will NOT get the glory. Remember, the Father is NOT in the midst of confusion. *For God is not the author of confusion, but of peace, as in all churches of the saints (1 Cor. 14:33).*

2. **Calm controlled behavior:** the ability to behave in a controlled and calm way even in a difficult or stressful situation.

A disciplined woman knows how to remain calm in the midst of difficult and stressful situations. She will not fall to pieces every time she faces adversity and stress. Her ability to remain calm will bring a calming reassurance to the people around her. A disciplined woman is not shaken by the things around her. She knows that God has her back and He will guide her through every situation. She also knows that no weapon formed against her will prosper. *"No weapon that is formed against you will prosper"* (Isaiah 54:17).

4. **Conscious control over lifestyle:** mental self-control used in directing or changing behavior, learning something, or training for something.

We must master the weights and bondages of our past. We must not allow the residue of our past to continually plague us and cause us to stumble and fall. If we cannot control our behavior, how can we tell others how to defeat the enemy who is constantly raging against them? We must possess the ability to direct or re-direct our past behavior onto a path that brings glory to the Father.

There is nothing more troubling and destructive than a woman who cannot control her appetites or lustful impulses. It does not matter whether the appetite or lustful impulse is sexual, physical, financial, emotional or mental, we must bring every lust, weight, snare and besetting sin under submission to Christ Jesus. Failure to do so will hinder or destroy your destiny.

Rabbit Trail: There are women going through life in the Second Timothy mindset:

For among them are those who worm their way into homes and captivate silly and weak-natured and spiritually dwarfed women, loaded down with [the burden of their] sins [and easily] swayed and led away by various evil desires and seductive impulses (2 Timothy 3:6 AMP).

The Apostle Paul calls them silly and weak-natured women who are weighed down by the burden of their diverse lusts and sins. These women are swayed and led by various desires and seductive impulses. The nature of the lust does not matter. Their lusts affect the triune woman: mind, body and spirit.

- Spiritually, they are dwarfed or stunted in spiritual growth and cannot advance any further than their lustful nature will allow. Sin keeps them from the presence of God, which hinders their ability to hear the voice of the Lord. The very nature of their sinful lusts render them unprofitable for the Master's use.

- Emotionally, they are tossed, driven by every wind of emotion, and live in their feelings. The spirit of offense is often in operation and uncontrollable because everyone hurts or maligns them in some twisted and perverse way of thinking.

- Sexually, they find it difficult, if not impossible to control the spirit of lust that drives their appetites. The Incubus spirit is often in operation within their sexual members. The Incubus spirit leads them to serve as temple harlots and no man or woman is off limits.

A Second Timothy woman will eventually burn out, run out or give out. She will have her hand in everything, but never capable of completing or accomplishing anything. She will use whoever is available in order to achieve her goals. Finally, a Second Timothy woman is HOT for whatever flavor of the week happens to stroll in her direction.

Why did I include this rabbit trail? Because a frontline woman must be in control of her members mind, body and spirit. You cannot have a woman standing on the frontline with her thighs twitching at the enemy because he is cute, bulging muscles and a sweet smile. We need women on the frontline who are in control of their lives and thighs because souls are at stake.

We must begin to address these issues because some of the biggest hypocrites and sexual deviants are operating in positions for which they are ill equipped. They cannot control their diverse lusts and impulses and as a result, they cannot stand as watchmen or gatekeepers because they are not strong enough to allow the power of God to keep them.

Once we apply these disciplinary actions to our lives, we will take on the characteristics or qualities that are vital to being a powerful tool for Kingdom advancement. A properly discipled woman must possess the following leadership qualities if she is to be the vessel prepared for the

Masters use. What are these qualities or characteristics?

➢ **Character:** *your public reputation or the set of qualities that make you distinctive, especially qualities of mind and feeling.*

➢ **Commitment:** *loyalty: devotion or dedication, e.g. to a cause, person, or relationship.*

➢ **Courage:** *the ability to face danger, difficulty, uncertainty, or pain without being overcome by fear or being deflected from a chosen course of action.*

➢ **Compassion:** *sympathy for the suffering of others, often including a desire to help.*

➢ **Competence:** *the ability to do something well, measured against a standard, especially ability acquired through experience or training.*

- ➢ **Convictions:** (1) ***firmly held belief:*** *a belief or opinion that is held firmly.* (2) ***firmness of belief:*** *firmness of belief or opinion .*
- ➢ **Charisma:** *the ability to inspire enthusiasm, interest, or affection in others by means of personal charm or influence*

Our goal as frontline women is to possess the qualities and attributes that are pleasing to the Father. We must begin and end with the seven C's listed above. Without them, we will falter and faint. We must have the strength to endure and overcome the temptations that are ever present tricks, traps or snares of the enemy.

Our final journey into the realm of discipleship involves our ability to endure the sufferings that accompany following the Lord's direction. We must possess the ability to endure hardships. Without this valued ability, we will faint at every wind, rain and tsunami that is thrown at us. The way we relate to "suffering" is a direct indication of how we view the sufferings of Christ. Because we belong to Christ, it is inevitable that His sufferings will overflow into our lives. As we share in His sufferings, we can expect His comfort and guidance to bring us through affliction and calamity. When we suffer the trials and tribulations of this present age, we must know with firm assurance that He is there to console and comfort us. We are partakers in His sufferings and we will also be partakers of His comfort and encouragement. *For just as Christ's [own] sufferings fall to our lot [as they overflow upon His disciples, and we share and experience them] abundantly, so through Christ comfort (consolation and encouragement) is also abundantly by us. But if we are troubled (afflicted and distressed), it is for your comfort (consolation and encouragement) and for your salvation; and if we are comforted (consoled and encouraged), it is for your comfort (consolation and encouragement), which works [in you] when you patiently endure the same evils (misfortunes and calamities) that we also suffer and undergo. And our hope for you our joyful and confident expectation of good for you is ever unwavering (assured and unshaken); for we know that just as you share and are partners in our sufferings and calamities, you also share and are partners in [our] comfort (consolation and encouragement) (2 Corinthians 1:7 AMP).*

Psalm 91 assures us that if we dwell in the secret place of the Most High, El Shaddai, we will abide under His Shadow. To abide means that we will find comfort, encouragement, strength, protection and more as we rest under His mighty shadow of protection. We are also assured that no evil will befall us and no evil will come near us. As His disciples, it does not matter what comes our way, He is there to lead, guide and protect us.

Finally, we are told in Second Timothy 2:12 that if we are willing to suffer with Him, we will also reign with Him, *"If we suffer, we shall also reign with him."* One thing is for sure, as disciples of Christ we will go through many sufferings in our life times. It is not about what you go through, what matters is how you go through it. In other words, do you go through your trial by fire murmuring and complaining or do you go through with you head up and your heart resting in the fact that the Lord will bring you through?

The one thing that will make your fire hotter and your season of affliction longer is murmuring and complaining. In fact, complaining will make the road a lot tougher to endure. God never receives the glory when we complain. Like a good soldier, we must endure the trials and come through the refiner's fire refined like pure gold. *That the trial of your faith, being much more precious than of gold that perisheth, though it be tried with fire, might be found unto praise and honour and glory at the appearing of Jesus Christ* (1Peter 1:7). Your trials are precious in the eyes of God, never take it for granted.

And I will bring the third part through the fire, and will refine them as silver is refined, and will try them as gold is tried: they shall call on my name, and I will hear them: I will say, It is my people: and they shall say, The LORD is my God

(Zechariah 13:9). The Lord is looking for a tried people who can stand in the midst of the fiery furnace of adversity and affliction. You are among the remnant that is being tried and refined as gold. We are a tried remnant that will stand, withstand and command.

Beloved, think it not strange concerning the fiery trial which is to try you, as though some strange thing happened unto you (1 Peter 4:12). Don't ever think that the Lord is not aware of your fiery trials; He knows what you are going through. He knows how difficult the journey is for you. He knows that it is a road that you must travel, if you are to become the Kingdom warrior that is needed in this season. Endure my sisters it will be worth it.

But rejoice, inasmuch as ye are partakers of

Christ's sufferings; that, when his glory shall be revealed, ye may be glad also with exceeding joy. (1 Peter 4:13). Rejoice because you have been chosen for a Kingdom assignment and know that to whom much is given, much is required. A great destiny requires great preparation. Long distance runners do not happen overnight, it takes years of training to enable them to go the distance. Pains, strains, heartaches and set backs are apart of the resistance training that they must endure. Look at your fiery trials as the resistance training that is preparing you for the journey ahead.

The day He reveals His plans for you, will be the day that you rejoice because you will realize that every heartache, set back and shut down was preparing you for a greater glory. Jeremiah 29:11 is a promise of your expected end. *"For I know the plans I have for you," declares the LORD, "plans to prosper you and not to harm you, plans to give you hope and a future* (Jeremiah 29:11).

The time of your revealing is at hand. Don't hinder the move of God by allowing the fleshly or carnal assaults to come against your destiny. The assaults will form, but the will not prosper unless you fall prey to the bait of Satan. Learn to endure like a good soldier and watch the Lord move on your behalf. You are called to be a frontline Kingdom woman with a frontline Kingdom agenda - walk in it.

Chapter 5

Are You a Kingdom Frontline Woman?

Are you a Kingdom woman ready to stand on the frontline? Do you know what it takes to be a Kingdom woman? I have outlined twenty-eight characteristics of a Kingdom woman based on Psalm 37. The complete list is in my book, *"A Woman of Worth: Dressed to Heal."* I pray that it will help you on your journey to becoming a Kingdom woman. A Kingdom woman is a frontline woman who is armed and dressed to heal a nation. It is time that you get in step with the Master for your frontline assignment.

Characteristics of a Kingdom Woman

There are twenty-eight characteristics of a Kingdom woman based on Psalm 37.[7]

1. She controls her feelings (v. 1, 7, and 8).
2. She is free from jealousy and envy (v.1).
3. She has absolute trust in God (v. 3, 5, & 40).
4. She is set apart to do good (v. 3).
5. She constantly delights in God (v. 4).
6. She maintains a life dedicated to God (v. 5).
7. She holds onto unwavering faith (v. 5).

8. She has total dependence on God (v. 7, 9, and 39).

9. She is free from anger and wrath (v. 8).

10. She walks in humility (v. 11).

11. She has an abundance of peace (v. 11).

12. She is content with her place in life (vv. 16-19).

13. She is unashamed in evil times (v. 19).

14. She is compassionate and giving (vv. 21-24).

15. She is obedient to God's directions (v. 23).

16. In hardships, the Lord is there for her (v. 24).

17. Her household is blessed (v. 26).

18. She walks in righteousness (vv. 21, 29, 30).

19. She possesses wisdom and justice (v. 30).

20. God's law is in her heart (vv. 31, 34).

21. She speaks truth and justice (v. 30).

22. She walks perfect and upright (v. 37).

23. She is a woman of peace & prosperity (v. 37).

24. She has the salvation of the Lord (vv. 39-40).

25. She stands firm in times of trouble (v. 39).

26. The Lord is her strength in trouble (v. 39).

27. The Lord is her help and deliverer (v. 40).

28. Her refuge is in the Lord (v. 40).

A Kingdom woman is a role model for other women. She possesses strength and qualities that bring glory to God. She is able to stand and withstand with dignity and honor. A Kingdom woman lives and breathes the Kingdom agenda. She is a consuming fire for the Lord and she will not compromise her stand for the Kingdom agenda. A Kingdom woman is also a Proverbs 31 woman with a mindset to walk in a spirit of excellence in every area of her life. *"Who can find a virtuous woman? For her price is far above rubies"* (Proverbs 31:10). She is clothed in strength and honor. *"Strength and honour are her clothing; and she shall rejoice in time to come"* (Proverbs 31:25). She is a wise and kind woman. *"She openeth her mouth with wisdom; and in her tongue is the law of kindness"* (Proverbs 31:26). She walks in excellence. *"Many daughters have done virtuously, but thou excellest them all"* (Proverbs 31:29).

It is important to know that you are a capable, intelligent and virtuous woman. You comfort and encourage, as you strive to do good in the lives of those around you. You are girded with strength: spiritual, mental, and physical. Your arms, like your heart are strong and firm. Strength and dignity are your clothing and your position is strong and secure. You are a woman who reverently and worshipfully fears the Lord, and for that, you shall be praised![8] You are a Kingdom woman of beauty, inside and out. As long as you walk in His power, authority, love, kindness and goodness, there is nothing ugly about you. It is not about the size of your waist, it is about the size of your heart.

You are a frontline woman who possesses power, authority, wisdom, honor and the peace of God. Woman of God, arise and take your rightful place among other frontline women. Look at the cover of this book and imagine yourself standing side by side with other frontline women. As you are standing, you are also commanding those things that are not as those they were (Romans 4:17 paraphrased). You are a frontline woman endowed with the power of the Living God. You are able to pull down strongholds and cast down every imagination that tries to exalt itself against the knowledge of who you know your God to be. When you have done everything, you know to do - you will stand on the strength of His word and His promises.

You are on the frontline and you must know without hesitation or reservation that no weapon that is formed against you will prosper. You are a mighty vessel for the Lord and there is no demon on the face of the earth that you cannot cast out as long as you walk in His power. No enemies of darkness can prevail against you as long as you stand on His Word and take the authority that is given to you by our Commander and Chief, Jesus Christ.

The kingdom of heaven suffereth violence, and the violent take it by force (Matthew 11:12 KJV). In other words, the Kingdom of heaven has been forcefully advancing, and forceful frontline women seize it by force as a precious prize, a share in the heavenly kingdom that is sought with most ardent zeal and intense exertion (Matthew 11:12 AMP paraphrased).

Our mandate is to advance the Kingdom of God, pursue and capture all for the King and the Kingdom. Just as King David inquired of the Lord regarding the pursuit of the troops that raided Ziklag, we must stay connected to the Lord when it comes to re-taking lands and territories for the Kingdom of God. *"And David inquired at the LORD, saying, Shall I pursue after this troop? Shall I overtake them? And he answered him, Pursue: for thou shalt surely overtake them, and without fail recover all"* (1Samuel 30:8).

Are you a Kingdom frontline woman? Yes and because you are a frontline woman, you must stay connected to the Captain of your soul for direction and guidance. You must prepare to advance without hesitation or reservation and without fail, you will recover all. Do not doubt who you are called to be for the Kingdom. Through your faith and belief in your calling, lies a strength that will take you all the way to victory.

I pray that this book is helping you realize your place of authority in the Kingdom agenda. God has anointed and appointed you for such a time as this. You are called by God to be a Frontline woman walking in the authority of:

- **A Warrior:** A woman who is experienced in spiritual warfare, who is ready, willing and able to pull down strongholds, and take authority in the name of Jesus.

- **An Overcomer:** You are an overcomer by the blood of the Lamb and by the very words of your testimony. Your testimony will help other women who have been through the fire or those who are currently in the fire.

- **A Disciple:** You are a follower who believes in and follows the teachings of our leader of Jesus Christ. As His disciple, you will go and make disciples of others.

Walk in your Kingdom authority with the Dunamis, Ischus, and Koach, Kratos or Exousia power of God. Each dimension of strength and power will enable you to do great exploits for the Kingdom of God and fulfill your Kingdom assignment.

- **Exousia** *(ex - oo - see - ah)* means the **authority** or right to act, ability, privilege, capacity, delegated authority. Jesus gave His followers Exousia power to teach, preach, heal and deliver. Exousia power gives you the right to walk Dunamis in power.

- **Dunamis** *(Du - na - mis):* the Greek word for power. Dunamis power is strength, ability, power that resides in you by virtue of the impartation made by Jesus Christ. It is also the power for performing miracles, moral power and excellence of your soul.

- **Koach** *(Ko - akh):* means vigor, strength force, capacity, power, wealth, means or substance. Generally, it means "capacity" or "ability" *But you shall [earnestly] remember the Lord your God, for it is He Who gives you power (KOACH) to get wealth, that He may establish His covenant which He swore to your fathers, as it is this day (Deuteronomy 8:18).*

- **Ischus** *(Is chus):* is Greek for **strength**. Many implications from health to moral endowment. Applied capacity or ability to perform.

- **Kratos** *(Kra tos):* is Greek for **might**. This is a word about power in action. It does not imply that action takes place, only that the power is ready to be used when needed.

Remember, there is no demon on the face of this earth that you cannot cast out as long as you walk in the authority and power of Jesus Christ. *"All authority has been given to Me in heaven and on earth. Go therefore…*(Matthew 28:18-20). This is your clarion call to go and take kingdoms, realms and spheres for the Kingdom of God. Go therefore, as you have been commanded, reclaim ground because He is with you always, even to the end of the age.

Chapter 6

Taking Back Ground

Now that we have established that you are a frontline woman who walks in the power and authority of the Lord, it is time to take back any ground that the enemy has manipulated from the hands of God's people. There are five aspects of reclaiming territory that we must address if we are going to repossess what the enemy has stolen from us. The five aspects include:

1. **We must recognize the resistance we will face on the frontline**. It is vital to recognize that you are going to face resistance from the enemy's camp. His soldiers are relentless when it comes to trying to discourage, distract or manipulate you into aborting your assignment. That is why it is imperative that you are well armed as you stand your ground. The Lord has equipped you with the tools necessary to accomplish His work and your charge is to stand and command, accessing the authority given to you by Christ Jesus.

2. **We must recognize that prosperity and wealth belong to us**. The Word tells us in Third John 1:2: *"Beloved, I pray that in all respects you may prosper and be in good health, just as your soul prospers."*

Prosperity comes in many forms, levels and dimensions. Never allow the enemy to box you in when it comes to the prosperity that is available to you. Prosperity flows through every area of your life: spiritual, physical, mental, emotional, relational and financial. Don't ever settle for prosperity in one area because it will cause a severe imbalance in your life. It is the Lord who is giving you the Koach power to make wealth, in order to confirm His covenant with you (Deuteronomy 8:18 paraphrased). Your covenant with Him will produce a wellspring of life in you. Remember His promise in Psalm 84:11: *"For the LORD God is a sun and shield; The LORD gives grace and glory; No good thing does He withhold from those who walk uprightly."*

3. **We must use the weaponry that is available to us**. When advancing for the Kingdom of God we must access the power that the Lord has given us. In the previous chapter, we discussed the different dimensions of power: Dunamis, Koach, Exousia, Ischus and Kratos. The Lord's power is the most formidable weapon we have when standing against the wiles of the enemy. Other weapons include the whole armor of God (Ephesians 6), prayer, rest, faith and peace.

4. **We must know the territories that are ours**. We must understand that there are lands, realms, territories and borders that the Lord has assigned to us and we are called to take dominion over them. For years, we have prayed the Prayer of Jabez

(1 Chronicles 4:10) asking the Lord to enlarge our territories. How many of us really understood what we were asking? There are realms and territories that are available to us as long as we walk in the power of God. Again, our ability to take ground revolves around our ability to walk in His power.

5. **We must walk in the authority that is ours**. *Jesus summoned His twelve disciples and gave them authority over unclean spirits, to cast them out, and to heal every kind of disease and every kind of sickness* (Matthew 10:1). *And Jesus came up and spoke to them, saying, "All authority has been given to Me in heaven and on earth"* (Matthew 28:18). *"Behold, I have given you authority to tread on serpents and*

scorpions, and over all the power of the enemy, and nothing will injure you" (Luke 10:19). You must recognize that Jesus has given you authority over ALL the power of the enemy. As long as you walk in the Lord's power, nothing will harm you. One morning while in prayer the Lord said, *"There is no demon on earth that you cannot cast out as long as you walk in my power."* Jesus has given us authority over unclean spirits, to cast them out, and to heal every kind of disease and sickness. We must walk in His authority if we want the world to witness His power and glory. *"These signs will accompany those who believe: In my name they will drive out demons; they will speak in new tongues; they will pick up snakes with their hands;*

and when they drink deadly poison, it will not hurt them at all; they will place their hands on sick people, and they will get well" (Mark 16:17-18).

What signs are following you? Whose power are you walking in? Are you accessing the power and authority that has been given to you by the Lord? Are you ready to stand and command in the army of the Lord? It is important that you walk in His power and authority. You are called to take lands, realms and territories for the Kingdom of God.

You are a frontline woman with the power of God flowing through your veins. As long as you walk in His power and authority, you will be a powerful force to be reckoned with. The kingdom of the enemy will come against you, but as long as you are well armed, the enemy must come under the submission of the power of God in you.

You must recognize and overcome the resistance you will face on the frontline. You must also realize that there are riches that belong to you and your holiness, righteousness and Kingdom authority will give you access to them. You must wield with precision the weapons that are available to you as you engage spiritual warfare. Finally, you must recognize that the realms that are yours will only be accessed through the authority that is given to you by the Lord.

Frontline woman, your time of revealing has come. If there are any doubts about your call to the frontline, stop, drop and pray. Seek the Lord for the direction of your assignment. Follow the Lord and you will never be led astray.

You are called to be a Deborah for this generation

and your ability to stand side by side with other frontline men and women of God is essential to your victorious purpose for the Lord. *"'Wake up, wake up, Deborah! Wake up, wake up, break out in song! Arise, O Barak! Take captive your captives"* (Judges 5:12). The Lord is calling us to wake up and break out in a song of victory because the battle is already won. There is something powerful about a song in the midst of the battle, it confuses the enemy. The days of cowering under the foot of the enemy are over. It is time to stand on the strength of God's Word, access His authority and walk in His power so that you can fulfill your Kingdom assignment.

As you walk out your Kingdom assignment stay in the presence of the Lord because that is where you will find all that you need to walk in victory. You will discover:

- Your marching orders so that you will not be misled by the enemy.

- Your peace when the battle is raging against you.

- Your joy and strength.

- Your light when the days look dark.

- Your healing when you have been wounded.

- Your shield and the lifter of your head.

- Your Rock that is higher than you are.

- Your help in time of trouble.

- Your hope and deliverer.

- Your shepherd and you shall not be in want.

- The restorer of your soul.

- Your guide in paths of righteousness.

- Your rod and your staff.

- Your comforter.

Frontline women, it is time to change the altitude of your environment and take a stand against the wiles of the enemy. It is time to bring anyone around you who has been walking in *low-level thinking* and *no level faith,* to an altitude of faith, trust and belief. It is time to step it up, get in line with other frontliners and raise the atmospheric pressure for the Kingdom.

You are a frontline woman and you possess the ability to bring others up a notch when they have a desire to step it up. You have the ability to bring others up to the Lord's standard, never allow anyone to bring you down. Frontline women never retreat when the enemy is advancing, it doesn't matter how much hell is breaking loose around you, don't ever back up. Frontline women when the need arises, forcefully advance for the Kingdom of God and do not shut down, break down or bow down to the enemy. You must know that the kingdom of heaven has endured violent assaults, and violent frontline men and women seize it by force, as a precious prize—a share in the heavenly kingdom that is sought with most ardent zeal and intense exertion (Matthew 11:12 AMP paraphrased).

When it is time to inquire of the Lord ask, "Shall I pursue this troop? Shall I overtake them?" Wait for the Lord to answer, when He releases you, pursue, overtake them and without fail recover all (1 Samuel 30:8 paraphrased and emphasis added).

Pursue with ardent zeal and intense exertion and you will capture and recover ALL. Stand your ground; take back ground and **RECOVER ALL**. Once you recover all you will understand the meaning of taking dominion.

Chapter 7

Taking Dominion

The day you realize what it means to take dominion will be the day that you will walk in the complete authority that has been given to you. In Genesis chapter 1 God created humankind and gave THEM dominion over all the earth. He did not give them partial dominion, He gave them dominion over ALL the earth. He did not give them temporary dominion, He gave them dominion over ALL the earth.

*And God said, Let us make man in our image, after our likeness: and let them have **dominion** over the fish of the sea, and over the fowl of the air, and over the cattle, and **over all the earth**, and over every creeping thing that creepeth upon the earth* (Genesis 1:26 KJV emphasis added).

*God said, Let Us [Father, Son, and Holy Spirit] make mankind in Our image, after Our likeness, and let them have **complete authority** over the fish of the sea, the birds of the air, the [tame] beasts, and **over all of the earth**, and over everything that creeps upon the earth* (Genesis 1:26 AMP emphasis added).

What is our mandate? Our mandate is to take

dominion over all the earth. God gave this directive to humankind and that means men and women are called to take authority over all the earth. God did not segregate or separate the mandate of taking dominion, He gave it to humankind, men and women. God made it very clear in His word, *"let them have dominion…over all the earth."*

As Kingdom men and women we must follow the directives of the Lord. One of His directives is to establish the Kingdom of God in the earth. In order to establish the Kingdom, we must take dominion or authority. When we walk in authority we won't have to make demands, our authority speaks for itself.

We are called to empower and transform lives in several ways.

1. Your daily walk will draw the lost.

2. Your overall lifestyle will capture the heart of those who are seeking authenticity.

3. The light you live will draw men out of darkness.

4. Your ability to bring life to the dead places will breath life into those who are spiritually dead.

5. Your battle cry of "leave no one behind" will guide you to impact the lost because you will give your ALL when it comes to taking it by force.

As you walk out your journey you will do so watching and praying for clarity of your kingdom assignment. Our culture must be transformed into a Kingdom culture if we are to impact lives and bring transformation to a dying world. It cannot be church as usual, otherwise generations will walk in darkness and we will find ourselves living Judges 2:10: *"There arose another generation after them who did not know the LORD."* We must not loose future generations to the hand of the enemy. His goal for our future is to steal and destroy our seed. The children are our seed and our future and we must protect them from the destructive devices of the enemy.

That is why we must stand as watchmen and gatekeepers of the Kingdom. Throughout the Bible the Lord set watchmen and gatekeepers to watch and defend the city. It does not matter where the Lord has positioned you as long as you take your position. Are you called to be a watchman? As a watchman your responsibility is the "man the watch" over the delegated assignment. *That's authority.* Are you a called to be a gatekeeper? As a gatekeeper your responsibility is to "keep the gates" opened or closed. *That's authority.*

Watchmen walk the wall to discern the atmosphere around them. Watchmen are frontline men and women who walk in a greater level of authority. Watchmen have a strong sense of discernment because he or she must be able to spot the enemy from afar. Unlike gatekeepers who only sees the enemy when he is at the gate, watchmen must be vigilant and on the alert.

Gatekeepers are similar to security guards who ensure that the enemy does not try to infiltrate the doors, portals or gateways. Gatekeepers ensure that no illegal access is gained by enemy combatants. Gatekeepers are armed with prayer and intercession and they can determine the threats against us. Several scriptures give us a glimpse into the level of responsibility watchmen and gatekeepers carry.

Watchmen

"Son of man, I have appointed you a watchman to the house of Israel; whenever you hear a word from My mouth, warn them from Me" (Ezekiel 3:17).

"I have posted watchmen on your walls, O Jerusalem; they will never be silent day or night" (Isaiah 62:6a).

Gatekeepers

After the wall had been rebuilt and I had set the doors in place, the gatekeepers and the singers and the Levites were appointed. "The gates of Jerusalem are not to be opened until the sun is hot. While the gatekeepers are still on duty, have them shut the doors and bar them. Also appoint residents of Jerusalem as guards, some at their posts and some near their own houses" (Nehemiah 1, 3).

But the four principal gatekeepers, who were Levites, were entrusted with the responsibility for the rooms and treasuries in the house of God. They would spend the night stationed around the house of God, because they had to guard it; and they had charge of the key for opening it each morning (1 Chronicles 9:26-27).

We can see from scripture that gatekeepers and watchmen carried a great responsibility in the Kingdom. As watchmen and gatekeepers, we have been entrusted with the responsibility for the House of the Lord. When was the last time you stationed yourself around the house of the Lord to guard it from the assaults of the enemy? When was the last time you spent 24, 48 or 72 hours shut in praying in the house of the Lord?

You are called to be a frontline woman and by the very nature of your calling, you are either a watchmen or a gatekeeper. It does not matter which one you are called to be, what matters is that you carry out the assignment and station yourself in prayer, fasting and seeking the face of God. What matters is that you take your charge seriously and bring glory to God.

When you take dominion over the things God has entrusted to you, you will see lives changed, hearts mended and nations healed. You must know your position in the Kingdom of God and avoid straying into other positions simply because they appear to be glamorous, receive accolades or financial gain. Your contributions to the Kingdom may go unnoticed for years, but fret not because the Lord will reward you in due season if you faint NOT. Don't ever give up on your destiny. You are on the edge of bringing to fruition your glorious destiny for the advancement of the Kingdom.

Frontline woman it is time to take your rightful place among other Kingdom warriors, overcomers and disciples and advance for the Kingdom of God. Go ye into all nations, bring healing to the nations and you will recover all. Be blessed.

About

The Author

About the Author

Dr. Jacquelyn Hadnot is an author, teacher and empowerment speaker whose passion is to empower lives through the Word of God.

God has called Dr. Jacquie to encourage, inspire, motivate and activate the gifts of the Spirit in order to raise powerful ministries in the body of Christ. She is becoming a voice on the subject of women's empowerment, prayer, worship and spiritual warfare.

She is a modern-day apostle with a strong prophetic and psalmist anointing. She has a revelational teaching ministry with a mandate to saturate the world with the Word of God. Jacquie's heart is to see people arise and walk in the destiny and inheritance of the Lord.

She founded It Is Written Ministries, a publication company, an accounting and consulting firm, and a global radio station. As a retired accountant and financial executive, Jacquie blends ministerial and entrepreneurial applications in her ministry to enrich and empower a diverse audience with skills and abilities to take kingdoms for the Lord Jesus Christ. She is a national and international lecturer, conference speaker, teacher, business trainer, and financial consultant. She also provides consulting services to businesses, churches and individuals.

She has written over thirty books, manuals, and other materials on intimacy with God, prayer, fasting and spiritual warfare. She has also released several music Cds and received numerous music and book publishing awards.

Beyond the pulpit, Jacquie is a talk-show host on both television and radio with her own programs; The Exchange and Light for Your Path, respectively. Weekly, she applies God's wisdom to today's world solutions. Her ministry goal is to make Christ's teachings relevant for today. She also publishes a quarterly magazine.

In addition to her vast experience, Jacquie has a Thd. in Pastoral Theology and a Masters in Ministry Leadership. She is also a wife, mother and grandmother. She and her husband, Minister Gregory Hadnot presently pastor It Is Written Ministries in Kansas City. They also serve as owners and officers of Igniting the Fire Media Group.

A Woman of Worth: The Movement

A movement of empowerment for the nations.

When a woman is healed, she can heal a nation.

A Woman of Worth: The Movement

We are a Kingdom-minded, Kingdom-oriented ministry with a mandate to encourage, empower and motivate women to walk in victory.

A Woman of Worth: Loving the Skin I'm In, hereafter referred to as AWOW is a gathering of women of destiny designed to encourage, inspire and motivate them to reach the destiny and purpose wrapped inside of them. *"For I know the plans I have for you," declares the LORD, "plans to prosper you and not to harm you, plans to give you hope and a future"* (Jeremiah 29:11).

It is time for women to reconnect with the woman God created them to be. For years, many women have been sitting on the back burner, side lined due to low self-esteem, insecurity and inferiority. Many are pregnant with gifts, talents, ministry, peace, joy, healing, praise, dreams, goals and purpose. God has placed "purpose" inside of us.

Our Goal

A Woman of Worth: Loving the Skin I'm In is more than a conference; it is an agent of change in the lives of God's people. Amidst life's labor pains, AWOW's goal is to show women that they have the inner-power to pursue their purpose. It is time to deliver their destiny and birth their dreams. They are often hearing negative and detrimental words that destroy their self-worth

Through the pains of emotional, physical and verbal abuse, many believe the report of the enemy and give up on accomplishing anything in life. Our vision is to empower individuals to reach their God given potential and release them from the bondage that has held them captive for so many years.

The bible says faith comes by hearing, and hearing by the Word of God. What are they hearing? Often they hear the same record repeating itself. A Woman of Worth is here to change the record and help our sisters hear a new sound. A sound released from heaven that sings, "You are a woman of worth, a treasure beyond price. You are the apple of God's eye and He has great plans for your life."

Services
- To motivate women to realize their purpose and fulfill their God-given assignments.

- To show women how to actualize their dreams through development of business plans, marketing strategies, vision plans and other key elements necessary for birthing their purpose.

- Teach women to maximize their gifts, ideas, talents and potential.

- Distribute food and clothing to families in need year round.

- Provide grants and scholarships to push them into their destiny.

Learn to love your authentic self:

- Move from low self-esteem to unshakable confidence.

- Stay positive and joyful in challenging times.

- Take responsibility for your life.

- Get better results in life by making better decisions.

- Identify priorities and create new choices.

- Take positive action to create change.

- Create a project plan with focus, commitment and motivation.

- Discover the knowledge and power to move life forward.

- Unlock their God given potential.

- Develop leadership skills.

We also provide assistance with other needs:
- Clothing distribution at most conferences.

- Food distribution at the conference.

- Grants or scholarships given at most conferences.

A Woman
of Worth:
The Series

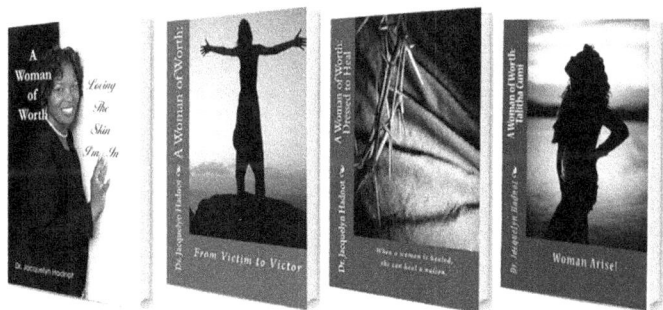

A Woman of Worth: The Books

A Woman of Worth is an eight (8) book series that takes you on a journey of discovery, encouragement and empowerment. Through this series, you will travel with Dr. Jacquie Hadnot along the road of devaluation, low self-esteem, domestic violence, healing and deliverance. Once healing and deliverance have taken place, the journey will continue as women discover the purpose and destiny awaiting them in the womb of destiny. As women arise from the pits of pain and despair, they will learn what it means to answer the call and commission of God. They will discover what it means to wear a mantle of authority as they walk into their Kingdom assignment.

Each book in the series takes the reader on a journey that is sure to bring fresh revelation, fresh vision and clarity of purpose. If you have a desire to live a life of passion, purpose and destiny, then this series is for you.

Book #1: *A Woman of Worth: Loving the Skin I'm In* addresses the issues of low self-esteem, devaluation, insecurity and inferiority. Learning to love the skin you are in is not always as easy as we think. In a society where we are judged according to our weight, height, skin color, careers or titles, the enemy can bring us to a place where we devalue or look down on ourselves. *Loving the Skin I'm In* takes you on a journey of discovering self-confidence, peace and inner strength. *Also available: A Woman of Worth: Study Guide & Journal*

Book #2: *A Woman of Worth: From Victim to Victor* addresses the issues of domestic violence and its effects on the lives the victors who overcome it. *From Victim to Victor* chronicles the story of a young woman caught up in the cycle of abuse. The book begins with Jayla's story and moves into the realities of today's society where abuse of women is at an all time high. Join Dr. Jacquie as she tells this heart-breaking story with truth and transparency. *Also available: An interactive Study Guide include in the book.*

Book #3: *A Woman of Worth: Dressed to Heal* follows the spiritual, emotional and physical healing of a woman as she answers the call on her life. *Dressed to Heal* takes you on the journey of a woman who is being used to bring healing to the nations. This book outlines the foundation, characteristics and seasons of a woman who is being dressed to heal, to heal a nation. When a woman is healed, she can heal a nation. *Also available: A Woman of Worth: Study Guide & Journal*

Book #4: *A Woman of Worth: Talitha Cumi* encourages women arise to the design and plan that God has for your life. For years, women have been on the backburner of mediocrity due to the issues of life. It is time to ARISE to a new life in Christ because there is an amazing destiny waiting on the other side of adversity, pain and affliction. It is time to arise, come together, lock arms and become the spiritual mothers, mid-wives, sisters and intercessors that are needed in this season. There is purpose, passion and vision waiting to be birthed from the womb of destiny. *Also available: Talitha Cumi! Journal*

Book #5: *Affirmations for a Woman of Worth: I Hope You Dance*, is a collection of prayers, affirmations and declarations for a woman of worth to pray over every area of her life. *Affirmations for a Woman of Worth* is an empowerment tool in a book to help women speak those things that are not as though they were. This book will create an atmosphere for birthing destiny through the power of the spoken word. This book contains over 250 affirmations to make a part of your everyday life as you find joy in dancing the dance of an over comer.

Book #6: *A Woman of Worth: From the Pit to the Promise* chronicles a woman's journey from the pits of poverty, despair, depression and suicide to become a woman of promise, passion and purpose. This book is for women who have been at the depths of despair, hopelessness and helplessness and on the verge of giving up. When a woman does not know the power locked inside, she will wallow in the pit of pity. Discover what it takes to go from the pit to the promise. *Also available: Pit to Promise Journal. (Available: 2014)*

Book #7: *A Woman of Worth: Mantle of Authority* discusses the mantle that God has placed on His women for their Kingdom assignment. We are "the called" in this season, but it is up to us to answer the call. We are given the vision, then the Lord issues the call and once we are prepared, we are given the commission to go forth as Kingdom woman and advance the Kingdom of God. *Mantle of Authority* uncovers the vision, the call and the commission of a woman of worth. (Available: 2015)

Book #8: *A Woman of Worth: Testimonies from the Threshing Floor* shares testimonies from thirty-one (31) women who have walked through the fire, floods and personal tsunamis of life. Each woman shares her testimony candidly as a means to encourage other women to walk in freedom. *Testimonies from the Threshing Floor* will leave you breathless waiting for the next sister to share her story. *Also available: Threshing Floor Journal (Available: 2015)*

Other Books & Materials by Dr. Jacquie

Books in Print

- ➢ The Art of Spiritual Warfare (2012) (Book & Journal)
- ➢ A Woman of Worth: Loving the Skin I'm In (Book & Journal)
- ➢ A Woman of Worth: Loving the Skin I'm In Study Guide
- ➢ A Woman of Worth: From Victim to Victor
- ➢ A Woman of Worth: Dressed to Heal (Book & Journal)
- ➢ A Woman of Worth: Talitha Cumi, Woman Arise!
- ➢ A Woman of Worth: Talitha Cumi Journal
- ➢ Affirmations for a Woman of Worth: I Hope You Dance
- ➢ Affirmations for a Woman of Worth: Study Guide
- ➢ Closing the Doors to Satan's Attacks: *Overcoming Fear*
- ➢ Trapped in the Arms of Death: *Overcoming Grip of Suicide*
- ➢ Your Declaration of Dependence on God
- ➢ In the Face of Adversity: *Overcoming Life's Storms*
- ➢ The Enemy in Me: *Overcoming Self-Life Issues*
- ➢ There's a Famine in the Land: *Overcoming the Great Recession*
- ➢ Ignite My Fire, Lord (Book & Journal)
- ➢ The Extravagant Love of God: Experiencing the Prophetic Flow
- ➢ Cry Aloud, Spare Not! A Prophetic Call to the Fast
- ➢ Cry Aloud, Spare Not! The Companion-Study Guide
- ➢ Standing for the King: While in the Spotlight of the Media
- ➢ Pretty in Pink: Praying Influential Nonsense Free Women
- ➢ Unlocking the Power to Get Wealth
- ➢ His Mercy Endures Forever: Psalms, Prayers & Meditations
- ➢ To Make War with the Saints: Satan's Kingdom Agenda
- ➢ A Treasure in the Pleasure of Loving God

- Loving God through His Names: 365 Days of the Year
- When Fear Crept In
- Deeper…
- Naked, Broken and Unashamed
- Where Is Your God? Have We Lost the Referential Fear of the Lord? (Coming 2015)

Audio Books & Teachings

- More of You… (Volume 1)
- In the Face of Adversity: Overcoming Life's Storms
- Be Not Deceived…
- Where Is Your God?
- Recognizing Your Due Season
- Praying the Healing Scriptures
- The Enemy in Me: Overcoming Self-Life Issues
- Trusting God in a Season of Discouragement
- The Harlot Heart

Music

- The Extravagant Love of God
- The Spoken Word of Love
- His Mercy Endures Forever: Praying the Psalms

DVD

- When Your Faith is Being Tested
- What Made David Run

➢ Agents of Change
➢ Virtuous Women of Worship
➢ Secrets of the Secret Place (4 volume series 2014)

TO CONTACT DR. JACQUIE:
www.jacquiehadnot.com

Or write us:
jacquie@jacquiehadnot.com
Booking@jacquiehadnot.com

Igniting the Fire Media Group
P.O. Box 25894
Overland Park KS 66213
www.ignitingthefire.net

You can do all things through Christ who strengthens you because you are more than a Conqueror.

You are a frontline woman: warrior, overcomer and disciple.

Bibliography

[1] Hans Kvalbein. Go Therefore and Make Disciples: The Concept of Discipleship in the New Testament. 1988.

[2] Hans Kvalbein. Go Therefore and Make Disciples: The Concept of Discipleship in the New Testament. 1988.

[3] Hans Kvalbein. Go Therefore and Make Disciples: The Concept of Discipleship in the New Testament. 1988.

[4] Hans Kvalbein. Go Therefore and Make Disciples: The Concept of Discipleship in the New Testament. 1988.

[5] Hans Kvalbein. Go Therefore and Make Disciples: The Concept of Discipleship in the New Testament. 1988.

[6] Hans Kvalbein. Go Therefore and Make Disciples: The Concept of Discipleship in the New Testament. 1988.

[7] Dr. Jacquelyn Hadnot, A Woman of Worth: Dressed to Heal, 2013.

[8] Dr. Jacquelyn Hadnot, A Woman of Worth Loving the Skin I'm In, 2012

JOURNAL

SPACE

JOURNAL SPACE

Frontline Women: Warriors, Overcomers & Disciples

150